CA$H IN ON
YOUR SKILLS

WAYS TO
MAKE MONEY WORKING WITH
YOUR HANDS

SIYAVUSH SAIDIAN

Enslow Publishing
101 W. 23rd Street
Suite 240
New York, NY 10011
USA

enslow.com

Published in 2020 by Enslow Publishing, LLC
101 W. 23rd Street, Suite 240, New York, NY 10011

Library of Congress Cataloging-in-Publication Data

Names: Saidian, Siyavush, author.
Title: Ways to make money working with your hands / Siyavush Saidian.
Description: New York : Enslow Publishing, 2020 | Series: Cash in on your
  skills | Audience: Grade 7-12. | Includes bibliographical references and
  index.
Identifiers: LCCN 2019012379| ISBN 9781978515581 (library bound) | ISBN
  9781978515574 (pbk.)
Subjects: LCSH: Manual work--Juvenile literature. | Self-actualization
  (Psychology)--Juvenile literature.
Classification: LCC HD4901 .S1625 2019 | DDC 650.1--dc23
LC record available at https://lccn.loc.gov/2019012379

Printed in China

To Our Readers: We have done our best to make sure all website addresses in this book were active and appropriate when we went to press. However, the author and the publisher have no control over and assume no liability for the material available on those websites or on any websites they may link to. Any comments or suggestions can be sent by email to customerservice@enslow.com.

Portions of this book originally appeared in *Money-Making Opportunities for Teens Who Are Handy* **by Philip Wolny**

Photo Credits: Cover Steve Debenport/E+/Getty Images; p. 5 Lisa F. Young /Shutterstock.com; p. 8 GeorgeRudy/iStock/Getty Images; p. 10 mooremedia /Shutterstock.com; p. 13 val lawless/Shutterstock.com; p. 15 Suwin/Shutterstock.com; p. 18 © iStockphoto.com/dolgachov; p. 21 © iStockphoto.com/pink_cotton_candy; p. 22 Aigars Reinholds/Shutterstock.com; p. 26 Koy_Hipster/Shutterstock.com; p. 29 © iStockphoto.com/fizkes; p. 32 © iStockphoto.com/MachineHeadz; p. 36 © iStockphoto.com/sturti; p. 39 Peshkova/Shutterstock.com; p. 41 Elnur/Shutterstock .com; p. 44 © iStockphoto.com/GCShutter; p. 46 © iStockphoto.com/Steve Debenport; p. 49 © iStockphoto.com/industryview; p. 52 © iStockphoto.com/jeffbergen; p. 53 Kathy Hutchins/Shutterstock.com; p. 55 © iStockphoto.com/wesvandinter; p. 59 © iStockphoto.com/SolStock; p. 61 © iStockphoto.com/AleksandarGeorgiev; p. 62 stoatphoto/Shutterstock.com; p. 64 franco lucato/Shutterstock.com.

CONTENTS

There are a lot of things teens like to do with their spare time. On the weekends, some friends may head down to the mall to hang out, walk around, and shop. Others may go throw a ball around at a local park, enjoying the weather without a care in the world. Still more could find themselves at the movie theater catching a Sunday morning matinee showing of the latest flick. Imagine, now, a girl who—instead—is working with her hands in her parents' garage, working on bicycles. She loves piecing things back together and learning how they work, so after saving up her allowance to buy some tools, she started offering to repair people's bikes for a small fee. Now, a year later, she has a booming business that is making her money, all while she works with her hands.

Doing something like fixing bicycles is just part of her business, however. A lot goes on behind the scenes. To keep track of clients, costs, and payments, she uses a spreadsheet program that she learned about in school. To drum up business, she takes some time after school to hang posters around town, and she is thinking of making a small advertising push on social media. A lot goes into running one's own business, but she is hoping that after a few more

From painting to landscaping and more, jobs working with your hands can be creatively and physically rewarding.

years of flying solo, she will have enough experience and skills to work at a local bike shop.

This is just one example of a handy teen using their skills and passion to make money at a part-time job. From self-employment to a job at a chain home improvement store, teens who are comfortable working with their hands—and good at it—have endless opportunities to make a little money, even if they can only work for a few hours a week. On top of that, there are countless volunteering opportunities and organizations that would welcome a handy teen with open arms.

Gaining experience as a teen—either for pay or on a volunteer basis—is a major part of joining the workforce as an adult. Working to learn the skills, discipline, and problem-solving abilities of a handy professional will go a long way in career preparedness across many different fields, including auto repair, carpentry, construction, electrical work, and many more.

On top of that, the experience of working with one's hands as a teen teaches valuable lessons about both time management and money management—which are incredibly helpful and rarely taught in public schools. A teen seeking full-time employment with a résumé that features their background in working with their hands will have a strong advantage over competitors. Though full-time employment is a long way off for a teen who is doing handy work after school hours, there is also an immediate satisfaction to the work. Teens who are good with their hands often enjoy the sheer act of figuring out how to put something together or repair something that was once broken.

Possibility within Reach

As the name implies, those who are handy are good at working with their hands—and this almost always goes beyond just the physical labor one might expect. The word handy also describes someone who is good at handling machinery, fixing things (including machinery), using tools to get something done, and so much more. This broad definition means that anyone who can exhibit those skills will be a valuable part of a family, company, or community.

Working with one's hands is a strong option for both short-term enjoyment and long-term expectations. Immediately, being handy is a skill that can bring in consistent money, even for a teen working part-time. In the long run, however, that money will not be nearly as valuable as the skills, experience, and lessons that are learned from rolling up one's sleeves and getting down to business. From master carpenters to advanced car technicians, leaders in skilled fields can almost always point to a childhood spent doing handy work. On top

There are countless fields that allow young people to earn money working with their hands. From carpentry to car repair, being handy is valuable.

of that, working with one's hands also presents the possibility of a future career in architecture, computer science, engineering, and many other industries.

A "Handy" Skillset

Handy people may realize early on that they are especially good at doing physical and technical tasks. Even very young children can demonstrate a true love of using tools and figuring out how the physical world around them works. Just as young writers or artists may start out writing in their diary or drawing, a handy kid might be fascinated with taking apart a telephone or other common household item—and figuring out how to put it back together.

Some teens may find out they like these kinds of hobbies more than artistic or other activities. They may even love creative pursuits, too. In fact, handy people also often show great creativity, imagination, and problem-solving skills through physical work. The two worlds are not exclusive.

Even if they do not pursue a skilled trade or technical career as adults, young people can use their special abilities to make money in many different ways. A good deal of them do not realize they have this talent until later in life because they do not try it out or do not have the opportunity. An insurance agent may realize at age forty that he loves woodworking and start a business making furniture, while an executive vice president might discover she has a hidden love of repairing and maintaining table lamps.

Always in Style

For those who have the talent and inspiration, being handy—and making some cash as a result— can be not only financially fulfilling, but also emotionally satisfying.

Although science and technology such as the internet have provided society with great convenience and connectivity, many feel alienated

Working with one's hands can be extremely rewarding, both professionally and personally. The end product of a handy person's day of labor is immediate and satisfying.

(or separated emotionally) from the work they do every day. While it is certainly not true for everybody, many workers feel disconnected from the technology that surrounds them in the workplace.

Some teens considering a future career may find the idea of sitting in an office cubicle or working in retail, for example, unattractive. As motorcycle mechanic and writer Matthew Crawford wrote for the *New York Times Magazine* in May 2009, "Working in an office, you often find it difficult to see any tangible [real] result from your efforts. What exactly have you accomplished at the end of any given day?" The manual arts allow workers to feel a physical connection to their jobs. Many find the physical results, such as a finished table or a working engine, very satisfying.

Crawford also pointed out that although many traditional office jobs sound great on paper, with high pay and opportunity for advancement into the future, these positions often come and go frequently, and the demands of these professions are constantly changing with the times. Physical, handy jobs, however, will always be there. "Now as ever, somebody actually has to do things: fix our cars, unclog our toilets, build our houses," Crawford observed.

In the last few decades, many jobs that used to be based in America are now carried out in foreign countries. This is a phenomenon known as outsourcing. A customer calling to ask about his or her internet or cable bill might speak to someone in a call center in India, for example.

If people need to fix a car, computer, or phone; have their house painted; or have a new kitchen or bathroom installed, they hire someone in their own town or city to do it. When a hurricane tears down thousands of power lines, skilled men and women must come in person to fix the electrical grid. It is impossible for these tasks to be done remotely, and for that reason, the people who have the skill to do these tasks are in high demand. Handy people's skills will always be necessary and cannot be outsourced.

Think of all things businesses and homes use. Now imagine all the trades associated with keeping them running smoothly: plumbers; mechanics; carpenters; furniture makers; construction workers; electricians; masons; heating, ventilation, and air-conditioning (HVAC) technicians; and field service technicians for cable, phone, and internet lines. Making money being handy in one's teen years can lead to rewarding, well-paid positions that will always be needed.

Times of Change

The Great Recession that began in 2008 in the United States and spread around the world left many people with fewer resources than before. People who once had hired someone to install a door in their home, clean their pool or mow their lawn, or do other basic jobs, suddenly did not have as much money as they used to.

Handyman-type tasks once performed by professionals were an unaffordable luxury for many as the recession continued. However, such changes open up a door of opportunity for young people who are handy. A neighbor in one's town can perhaps not afford to pay a landscaping company to keep the yard trimmed and neat. Maybe a handy teen can step into this niche and start their own neighborhood lawn service. The same holds true

Though some teens may be intimidated by a yard like this, there is good money to be made in landscaping for people who do not have the time or energy to maintain their own lawn.

13

for home improvement, automobile service, and other types of maintenance.

In better economic times, a person may simply throw out an old television, piece of furniture, or other household item and buy a new one. When money is tighter, a handy young person can repair such items for less than a professional service might charge.

Changing Back?

Teens choosing skilled trades, manufacturing, and other physical labor may be in luck in the 2020s and beyond. Alan Brown, writing for the American Society of Mechanical Engineers (ASME) in March 2011, cited studies that showed that a majority of American teens were uninterested in the manual arts: less than 30 percent were enthusiastic about such careers. Also, fewer adults nowadays enjoy working with their hands, even at home as a hobby.

This seemingly bad news is actually good news for handy teens, whose skills will be more in-demand than ever before because of a labor shortage in technical fields. For years, high school students have been losing enthusiasm for such work. Industry leaders blame the fact that vocational classes have been cut over time. As school budgets have been reduced and curricular standards have changed over time, fewer and fewer high schools have been offering programs that allow students to see into the world of working with one's hands. As a result, it is hard to get teens interested in these businesses.

Many young people see working with their hands as unglamorous, uncool, or beneath them. Fighting this perception can bring interested youths into the field, as can reminding them that these jobs can be

Though many young people do not realize it, the manufacturing industry has become high-tech and exciting with the rise of robots and computers in the twenty-first century.

as well paid and challenging as others. There is often a perception—even among educated adults—that jobs in an industry such as manufacturing should only be taken as a last resort. Some even believe that jobs that involve working with one's hands are less valuable than traditional office employment. These perceptions could not be any further from the truth. Skilled manufacturers and people with handy skills are responsible for keeping the economy running and making sure people have safe, effective access to goods and services.

The World Is Yours

One of the best things about being handy is the opportunity to be one's own boss. Handy teens sell their skills and abilities. They can set their own hours, working around their school and personal schedules. Valuable lessons to learn through self-employment include time management, scheduling, and keeping track of money.

Depending on how handy or accomplished someone is, that person might not find paying work right away. One way to gain valuable experience and skills is to intern or volunteer. A teen interested in bike repair might be able to get free training by volunteering at a bike shop in exchange for

HELP IS HARD TO FIND

With the rise of industries related to technology has come a drop in young people interested in taking on handy work. While tens of millions of high schoolers are encouraged to earn bachelor's or more advanced degrees, many jobs that would involve working with their hands—such as construction work, electrical work, and ironwork—are going unfilled. An article by Ashley Gross and Jon Marcus featured on NPR revealed some of the hidden truths about the skilled labor industry.

While an entry-level traditional office position might have dozens of qualified applicants, a similar job as a contractor will have none. In fact, it has been reported that 70 percent of American construction companies have trouble filling openings. Though many people think this is because these jobs do not pay well, nothing could be further from the truth. NPR's article closely examined this lack of handy work interest in Washington—and found that many of the jobs that could not be easily filled would pay more than the state's average wage of $54,000.

inexpensive or free bike parts, for example.

Various organizations, including community groups, charities, and religious organizations, might have similar opportunities for a handy teen to build his or her résumé. While giving back to the community, she or he can build confidence and skills that can soon result in paid opportunities.

Being good with one's hands opens up a world of money-making possibilities. However, a lot more goes into skilled handy jobs than just the physical work components. Tracking one's finances; becoming familiar with labor laws for minors; education in safety and technical skills; and developing the habits needed for working for oneself (and others) are all

Volunteering to do some hands-on labor not only helps the community, it is also a good way to see if this kind of work is something worth pursuing as a career.

important parts of the process.

Figuring out what to do is a good start. In an increasingly technological world, handy skills are in demand. Televisions, computers, bikes, and countless other items with working parts need repair and maintenance. Even jobs that seem straightforward benefit from a skilled worker, such as painting, maintaining pools and yards, window washing, and cleaning houses. Someone might spend an afternoon waterproofing a deck, fixing a toaster oven, designing and building signs for neighborhood customers, or cleaning gutters on houses.

When in doubt, figuring out what young people enjoy most will lead them to jobs and tasks that are satisfying, as well as lucrative. Money-making opportunities exist everywhere for teens who are handy. The only limits are one's creativity, open-mindedness, and talent.

Reaching Out

While there are unquestionably a lot of advantages to being self-employed, there are also a lot of reasons to seek out employment from a company. It is easier to find a job, the market is already established, and the pay comes from a stable source that is unlikely to stop abruptly. While the lessons to be learned from starting one's own business are invaluable, there are also bonuses that come along with learning from someone else. There are countless jobs available that involve working with one's hands, and handy teens have an increased chance of landing these jobs over other young people who are not used to—or interested in—doing physical labor.

Friendly Faces

For someone handy, there are many employment options out there. These may depend on where the person lives and how close and plentiful the jobs are—for example, right in his or her neighborhood. It can sometimes be easier to find work for neighbors, as they will be familiar with the young person they are hiring.

Though it may seem old-fashioned, selling services door-to-door can be a great way for a young person to find work, especially if the neighbors are family friends.

A teen worker who lives hot and dry region might apply for after-school or summer work in pool service. Workers as young as twelve can master brushing, cleaning, testing water chemistry, and basic pump maintenance. Looking up pool service companies online—some of which even offer courses and certifications in basic pool maintenance—is a good idea. People will want someone who knows that they are doing; taking care of pools is a lot of work, after all.

Coastline Cruising

The same job-seeking approach works for those who live near ocean coastlines, rivers, lakes, and other waterways popular with tourists and leisure seekers. Keeping in mind age and safety restrictions for their

Keeping in mind age and safety restrictions for their age groups, teens should take advantage of local maritime (sea-related) opportunities. Beach and tackle shops may need help during busy seasons, for example.

Others can go for positions at places that rent out boats and recreational vehicles, where they can get exposure to engines, basic maintenance, and other aspects of the trade. Yet another possibility is seeking work at marinas and docks, where tasks might include helping to clean and maintain boats, docks, and other facilities, or renting out equipment.

Lawn Warrior

Wherever there are private homes, clients need lawn and garden maintenance, also called landscaping. Although such a job may seem easy on paper, it is often physically demanding and requires

Instead of paying high prices for professional lawn care services, many neighbors would be happy to pay a teen to take care of their yards at a reasonable rate during the summer.

using complex tools. In most cases, teens must be at least sixteen years old to operate power (electric) tools like lawn mowers, trimmers, or weed cutters. Even underage teens familiar with such equipment from home use cannot be hired for these tasks. Such laws apply to many different workplaces and are meant to prevent injury (or death) to inexperienced young people. It is important to keep in mind all the rules and regulations when seeking employment.

Repair (Don't Replace)

Another job option is working in businesses that concentrate on helping customers and clients with mechanical repairs and maintenance. A bicycle shop, for instance, is a great place for teens to use and build their skills, especially if they are into cycling. Even a younger worker who may not be able to handle some of the more complex tasks (or cannot do so legally) can absorb useful experience by watching closely and asking questions.

Another similar job opportunity is working at an electronics retail store or repair service. Handy teens might have skills in both electronics and hardware and software and can build a résumé handling the small interior components and user-oriented side of computers, mobile devices, televisions, stereos, and almost any other type of consumer electronics. One advantage is that most such positions do not involve the use of heavy machinery or other complex equipment that teens cannot legally operate. Most tools used in electronic repair work are small and specialized to work with the components of the world's tiny gadgets. Much like working at a bike shop, another plus is learning under older, more experienced workers who can train teens in both the mechanical and administrative aspects.

Working Up

It may seem that younger, yet able, teen workers are at a disadvantage in such jobs, even if they are handy and passionate about the work. However, proving themselves talented and able-bodied will often quickly gain the trust of supervisors and business owners. Teens who build goodwill and experience and stay at a job for a while— throughout their high school years, for example—will receive promotions and raises and be able to handle increasingly more advanced responsibilities and equipment as they hit sixteen and seventeen years of age. They also put themselves first in line for being hired when they finish school and are looking for full-time jobs.

In the skilled manual trades, learning and developing useful money-making skills takes time. As with retail or other service jobs, young people will almost always start at the bottom. A beginner carpenter—sometimes called an apprentice—for example, may begin learning his or her trade in high school, or on the job, but typically must wait until the age of eighteen to really start working.

However, teens can apply for construction work or other junior positions in the trades even if they are too young to perform the tasks of older workers. These can include simple jobs like carrying heavy loads, being in charge of tools and supplies, preparing materials, making measurements or doing calculations, and doing paperwork and bookkeeping. Workers under age eighteen often get their big break by helping out in the office. Showing a friendly, eager face around any company is a good way to get noticed and gain respect.

Even a simple errand, such as visiting the hardware store, can be educational. It familiarizes the employee with the names, uses, and prices of specialized equipment and supplies. By proving himself or herself competent at the bottom of the ladder, the employee will gain the trust and respect of older coworkers. With these good relationships, senior employees will be that much more likely

There are countless types of tools, tool manufacturers, and tool applications. Knowing when to use what is an important part of any handy job.

to help a young person along with training and more responsibility.

While on a jobsite, there are two kinds of readily available information for a novice worker: information that is directly taught by a supervisor, and information that is gained by watching others work. Equally important, however, is the information that can be learned by asking questions, such as the following:

- Why are these nails good for this type of job? Why not use screws here?
- How durable is this material? Is it better for interior or exterior use?
- Why is this tool more expensive, and what is it for? Can this job be done with a different tool?

Young workers should also engage the different types of older workers they encounter, politely interviewing people in different trades if possible. This is one great way to figure out what subcategories of the trades interest them most.

Local and Chain Work

Another job possibility is working at a hardware store, either one that is locally owned or a national chain. If young people know about hand and power tools, paint, electrical supplies, plumbing necessities, and other home-improvement goods, it is a fantastic environment to earn cash and help others with their needs. Workers at these stores learn customer service, bookkeeping, and other administrative tasks, including how to use a store's computer system. Nowadays, these skills translate well to future jobs in any field and can provide a foundation for those who want to start their own business one day.

foundation for those who want to start their own business one day.

A job at a hardware store can also greatly expand their abilities as salespeople and their knowledge of a wide variety of goods. Hardware stores commonly reflect their geographical areas. For example, a seaside town's store might have marine and boating gear, while one in a farming area will offer a greater selection of agricultural supplies. Hardware stores are central to any community, and workers can make good contacts with neighbors and customers. One financial benefit is the chance to get goods at a deep discount, or for free, for oneself or one's family.

Grabbing a Job

Getting a first job requires a lot of effort. Step one is putting together a résumé. This is a document that any job seeker must email, mail, or otherwise submit to a company. A résumé provides contact information, work history, and other important details that will make employers want to hire that individual.

A professional résumé will have a teen's work record, including personal accomplishments relating to the job applied for, and any relevant school coursework listed. For example, teens should include metal or wood shop classes they have completed and any similar training they have received from others.

An applicant's résumé is the first thing an employer sees, so it is important to list any skills, experience, and knowledge that could be relevant to the job at hand.

It may also be useful to include any self-taught skills that show potential employers that they are handy. To develop or improve a résumé, teens can consult parents or family members, check online for the many resources available there, and seek the advice of school guidance and employment counselors.

Checking employment websites is crucial for anyone looking for a job. Online search engines allow users to find local job openings. Even if a position looks unattainable, it is important to apply to as many interesting jobs as possible. After all, the more résumés someone sends, the better the chance that potential employers will respond.

Other resources to search for jobs include websites for local state departments of labor and the U.S. Department of Labor. Various public and private organizations and programs exist that specialize in promoting teen employment, too. Searching for or directly contacting community-based organizations, religious groups, and other nonprofit organizations can also provide leads. Cities and states sponsor many youth employment programs, especially summer jobs programs, many of which include job training. It is a good idea to apply early in the year for programs that begin at the start of summer vacation.

Rubber Meeting Road

Teens should not only look online for jobs, but also visit actual places of business to apply in person. Businesses where this might be possible include offices and stores, both major chains and privately owned businesses. Other options might include local construction companies and businesses in the manual trades, retail and wholesale equipment sellers and repair shops, large chain stores that need handy employees, and many more.

BEING A GOOD INTERVIEWEE

Getting called into a business for an interview is typically a good sign for anyone who has applied for a job. Interviewers typically like what they have seen on an applicant's résumé, and the interview is a part of the hiring process in which they get to put a face to the name. While an interview can be highly stressful, it is important to keep some things in mind:

- Research the company and the position being offered.
- Look up common interview questions and practice responses to them.
- Lay out an interview outfit the night before so it is ready to go.
- Arrive a little early (five to ten minutes) to the interview.
- Have a positive attitude, good manners, and enthusiasm.
- Answer every question honestly—never lie or hide the truth.
- Prepare a few questions for the interviewer.
- Avoid taking too many pauses in responding to a question.
- After the interview is over, sent a thank you email to the interviewer.

Appearing in person—dressed appropriately and professionally, and with a positive attitude—shows bosses and hiring managers that a job seeker is serious and eager for work. They are more likely to remember a teen who shows up in person than the dozens or hundreds of applicants who only email or apply online.

Networking is another crucial part of job seeking. It is very important to keep eyes and ears peeled for word of potential job openings from one's relatives, family friends, and even parents of friends or acquaintances. Teens should contact members of their professional or social network as often as possible to expand their employment possibilities. Reaching out through social media can also help.

Often, it is these personal connections that count, mainly because there is otherwise little difference among young candidates for these jobs. All things being equal, a company will hire

Being a good interviewee is an art, but the most important things to bring to an interview are a positive attitude, a can-do mentality, and a willingness to do the job.

a son or daughter of an employee or someone they know. For instance, local summer jobs in construction might be hard to get. Even someone handy might not convince a hiring manager that he or she is right for the job. A teen whose uncle works as an overseer for the construction company, though, can set themselves apart from the rest and land the position.

What one knows is equally important as whom one knows when it comes to being on the job, however. Lazy, clumsy, or incompetent workers who are unwilling to learn or have a bad attitude will not last long. They are easily replaced.

Beyond just a résumé, teens should show up to interviews and places of business dressed professionally. This mode of dress can mean a button-down shirt, tie, and slacks or pants for boys, and a skirt or suit and blouse for girls. In many cases, business casual is enough for certain summer or retail jobs—a tucked-in polo shirt and khaki pants, for example. Go conservative: avoid oversized clothing or sagging pants, clothes that are revealing like short skirts or shorts, wild hairstyles, sweatpants or other athletic gear, and T-shirts and jeans. Even if the on-the-job dress code is very casual, job seekers should dress to impress—that can make all the difference when it comes to filling an open position.

Be Your Own Boss

Getting a lot of experience working for others is both useful and common, but working under someone else and being part of a large company is simply not the right fit for everyone. Some people may not like taking orders all day, or maybe they simply do not like the type of projects to which they are being assigned at a company. Maybe there are interpersonal issues at hand, or maybe they did not get the promotion they were aiming for. In all of these cases, an employee from a larger business might decide to walk away and form their own.

It is also possible that nearby companies are simply not hiring—so the only way to make money is to open one's own business and be her or his own boss. People who start their own small business are commonly called entrepreneurs, and there is a lot of opportunity for a young person who seeks that path. Though there are risks to entrepreneurship, there are also great rewards for teens who have passion, ambition, and talent with their hands.

DIY

Rather than waiting for work from others, do-it-yourself (DIY) teens create their own opportunities. They may already know how to maintain a bike; paint a wall; fix a television, computer, or mobile device; or build wooden shelves for their bedroom. They have found that the best way forward is learning by doing.

Just as writing, mathematics, or drawing get easier with practice, so does being good with one's hands. The better someone becomes at something, the easier it is to translate those skills into money-making opportunities. In many cases, it takes only a little bit of money for an industrious teen to start a small business.

Iron Things Out

Not everyone who is handy has a clear idea of what kind of business to start. Those interested in working with wood might find they have a particular talent for making birdhouses, furniture, or custom-made chess sets or other games. A cyclist or skateboarder may try his or her hand at bike repairs or using their paint and graphic design talents to design skateboard decks.

Even something as commonplace as bicycle repair can be a good starting point for a handy young person.

Whatever one's passion or talent, the resources to get started are out there. They exist online and as physical books and manuals. Schools often have elective classes that can help students discover and develop their talents. If they have the means, parents can help by enrolling children in private lessons or even finding a summer camp that has classes in arts and crafts and similar disciplines.

With some free time and dedication, a mechanically oriented person can get much of what she or he needs inexpensively and often for free. Visit local business owners and other people in the local area. Chances are that someone is throwing something away or that learning materials are just taking up space in someone's filing cabinet or closet.

More than any other possible resource, the internet has the easiest-to-access and largest collection of materials any handy person could hope to find. Online communities for engineers, mechanics, and many other types of tradespeople have countless free manuals, textbooks, and instructions available for legal download, and many times these are available at no cost. Everything a young person needs to get started may be just a click away.

If all else fails, someone who loves to tinker can buy cheap items at a thrift store or find items along the street on trash day. Yard or stoop sales can also be a gold mine for a handy teen. Basements, garages, and attics are great places to discover broken or forgotten furniture, toys, appliances, and other items to try one's hand at fixing or modifying. Remember, however, that parents should always give permission first; they are better able to decide if something is safe to buy or take home.

First Steps

Many entrepreneurs start small. Imagine a young teen that began learning woodworking at age ten, inspired by his father, a carpenter. His first "jobs" were small, simple furniture items given out as birthday and holiday presents, like foot stools and picture frames. Within two years, he gained the confidence and skill to make larger, more complicated pieces, like a chest of drawers or a dining room table and chairs.

With his parents' support, this teen decided to get serious and turn his hobby into a job. He began by using his father's tools and supplies. Using his computer, printer, and stationery supplies, he made business cards and flyers. He posted these flyers around the neighborhood and on the bulletin board at school, and handed business cards out door-to-door. Thinking creatively, he put them in local shopping areas and near malls and asked other businesspeople, such as doctors and real-estate agents, if he could leave materials for their customers to look over.

Online, he sent emails out to everyone he could and asked his parents and siblings to do the same. Taking good, clear pictures of his creations, he put up free advertisements on community and classified websites. He set up accounts on Facebook, Twitter, Instagram, and other social media networks. These

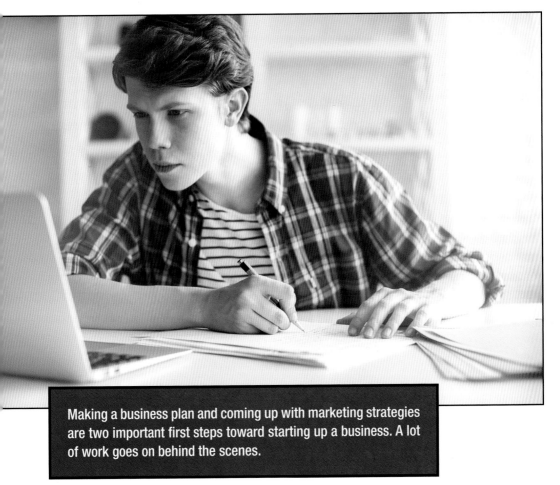

Making a business plan and coming up with marketing strategies are two important first steps toward starting up a business. A lot of work goes on behind the scenes.

networks helped grow his audience from only a few family members and friends to hundreds of potential clients around his city.

Handy Administration

There were limits to how much this teen could expand the business, however. Sitting down with his parents, they agreed that he would limit his work to a maximum of two or three hours a day and only three out of five school days, plus five hours a day on weekends. They all admitted that balancing schoolwork, other activities, and free time with his entrepreneurship would be best. During summer vacation, he expanded his hours to five days each week and took more orders.

With these limits in mind, he made sure not to promise customers too much, too soon. He kept his prices lower than a furniture store might charge and figured out realistic timeframes for filling orders. Customers were rarely unhappy with the finished product; he learned how to renegotiate prices and give discounts when necessary.

Early on, this teen craftsman also realized that he would have to keep track of his expenses and earnings. With resources like free, open-source software and books borrowed from the library, he taught himself some basic accounting and spreadsheet skills.

Under expenses, he made sure to keep track of all receipts for wood, paint, varnish, tools, and other purchased supplies, plus bus fare and other transportation costs. Slowly, he bought his own tools so he did not have to rely on his father's. Paid and unpaid invoices were stored on his computer and printed and stored in folders. When he had

No business—big or small—can survive without detailed records and accurate accounting. It is important to take notes, keep all receipts, and stay on top of paperwork when running a business.

the money, he took whatever extra courses he could to improve his abilities. Like many small businesspeople, he opened up an online payment account because it was the best way for him to safely perform online business transactions, as well as creating a joint checking account with his parents.

Though everyone's path to entrepreneurship is different, this example is one common method by which a young person can turn a hobby into a career. The precautions that must be observed when a teen starts their own business—such as setting expectations, monitoring work hours, and balancing work, school, and life—are always important.

Get the Word Out

Much like getting a job as someone else's employee, making money as one's own boss requires networking. It actually requires more (and nonstop) networking. A teen landing a job can rest easy for a while, knowing that they will have steady work and a steady income. A handy teen with his or her own business, however, often needs new customers and business contacts to keep busy and earn more cash.

Some types of work require more networking than others. A furniture maker might gain enough clients to last him or her a long time. A freelance bike mechanic may need more customers every month or year and must continue to hustle for them. If you work for yourself, you will come to realize how much of your time and effort should go to gaining new customers. This will also depend on how busy you want to be or how much time you can actually commit.

Any serious young entrepreneur these days should have some kind of online presence. Instagram, Twitter, and other social networks are

HANDY PROFILE: A TENNESSEE TEEN

While most people probably associate working with their hands with hard, physical labor, there are also skilled artisans whose work is detail-oriented and done manually. One example of a successful—and skilled—young entrepreneur is Moziah "Mo" Bridges, whose fashionable neckwear brand, Mo's Bows, is worth hundreds of thousands of dollars.

Bridges, who has loved to dress up in suits and ties since he was very young, started his company by designing and sewing unique and high-quality bowties from his own home at age nine. After dealing his handmade creations locally, he eventually broke into the national spotlight by appearing on shows as diverse as *The Steve Harvey Morning Show* and *Shark Tank*. With the added exposure from those shows, Mo's Bows has expanded from his hometown Nashville, Tennessee, into a recognizable brand with yearly revenues in the hundreds of thousands.

just the beginning. A quick video of fixing a bike, with before and after footage, uploaded to YouTube can be a great promotional tool, for instance. One idea is to maintain and update a blog that describes daily activities in one's field. It may just yield some new friends with common interests, but might also draw in new customers. Keeping up with what others are doing also gives teens new ideas and tips on how to improve their own work, including following the blogs of both older professionals and young novices.

Customer Is King

A satisfied customer or client is one of the best forms of advertising. Providing customers with extra business cards, flyers, and other promotional materials will make it that much easier for them

More than simply a way of sharing contact information, handing out business cards makes a young person look prepared, professional, and mature enough to handle a job.

to refer friends, family, and other colleagues. In addition, make it clear to them that they can always get in touch for other work or if they have questions or problems with work already performed or with items they bought. Answer any emails or calls or texts as quickly as possible, whether they are from existing clients or possible new ones. Entrepreneurs who act fast show others that they are professional and eager for work.

A Few Good Ideas

A popular and easy-to-start business is running a car washing, waxing, and detailing service. Cleaning supplies are relatively inexpensive, and nearly any urban or suburban area will provide plenty of clients. Assuming teens can get enough customers, it is also a good choice for two or more teens working together.

Another step is to add other auto-related services if someone on the cleaning team has the skills. These can include changing the oil and replacing fluids, filling tires with air, visual inspection, or stereo and speaker repair, installation, and adjustment.

There are many other ideas for starting one's own business. What type of business to run will depend on many factors and a teen's personality. If the person prefers working home alone, she or he can repair or build items at home, from a basement,

Opening up a weekend car wash could be a great way for a group of friends to earn money working with their hands—especially in a suburban area, which is sure to have plenty of clients.

garage, or backyard. Others might enjoy working outside: garden and lawn care, pool maintenance, and other outdoor activities might be best.

Teens who prefer visiting customers in their own homes might perform repairs or other handy work by advertising that they do house calls. One idea is to market services to senior citizens, many of whom are homebound and cannot do such work themselves. Others might be good salespeople and sell their products door-to-door, or rent space at public outdoor areas like flea markets to sell handmade creations.

Other entrepreneurs can make it big by thinking of a new, original idea. Marysville, Ohio, resident Hart Main started ManCans in 2010 after realizing that he could make and sell candles for men. By age thirteen, he was filling hundreds of orders every week for uniquely scented "man candles" with smells like sawdust, campfire, and bacon. He started small by making the candles using soup cans, designing his own labels, and dealing personally with his label and packaging suppliers. While his mother helped him with the wax, he was running the company himself as a teenager.

The story of ManCans did not stop there, however. After manufacturing more than 1,000 candles by hand in his home, the business was successful enough that Main hired some employees and rented out a warehouse space to fulfill his orders. In 2014, the Beaver Creek Candle Company took over the manufacture and distribution of Main's candles— including a SheCans line of candles with more feminine scents—which freed him up to finish high school and look toward the future. His story is one of enormous success, and it all came from working with his hands from his home.

Self-Improvement

The job market—both in the United States and around the world—has always been extremely competitive. With the rise of greater technology and increasing globalization, a single open position at a desirable company may have hundreds of applicants that come in from dozens of countries—all of whom are well qualified to take on the role. Automation—meaning robots taking the place of humans in certain jobs—is also a threat to an aspiring employee, as many industries have scaled back their human labor force in favor of more cost-effective automated methods.

This is not great news for teens who are looking for part-time or summer work. Because there are many applicants and not as many jobs, young people are often faced with competition from older, more experienced workers for entry-level positions. However, starting young has its benefits, as well. Starting to apply one's networking and business skills as a teen will help produce a strong résumé when it does come time to enter the serious job market after high school or college.

CHAPTER FOUR

Interning and Volunteering

In a highly competitive landscape, handy teens looking for opportunities often must adjust their expectations. Internships and volunteer positions are often good alternatives to paid work. Internships are junior positions in companies—mostly unpaid—that help younger workers gain experience and

Internships and apprenticeships are tried-and-true methods for getting one's foot in the door at many companies. Businesses are more likely to hire someone they know.

49

connections. Companies often hire their unpaid interns as paid employees after they spend some time with the business. This makes internships excellent for getting one's foot in the door.

Getting a spot in one of the growing number of training programs out there is also a way to gain valued skills. Leaders in manufacturing, skilled trades, and other physical professions are expanding these programs for young people because they are finding it hard to hire skilled workers that will stick with the company. Participating in one often leads to paid positions, especially through school and industry partnerships that help place candidates who are handy.

Nowadays, money is harder to come by for many businesses and private and public organizations and institutions, including charities, community groups, and faith-based organizations. This makes it even more important that they take advantage of the many teens out there who still need something to do after school or during the summer and are eager to learn, even if they do not earn a paycheck. It can be a win-win situation for both sides.

As with looking for paid work, teens should start early, especially for summer positions and slots. Begin searching online and in the community in the fall or winter, months before the positions actually open up. Deadlines may be set months in advance, and candidates need enough time to prepare, fill out any paperwork, and get personal recommendations, if necessary.

Teens with work or volunteer experience should ask employers and supervisors to write letters of reference, including current contact information. Applicants should not put all their eggs in one basket, so to speak, but instead try for many different opportunities. The more they research and apply, the better their chances of landing something, even if it is not their first choice.

A WOMAN'S TOUCH

Women workers are underrepresented in many fields, and while that is rapidly changing in STEM (science, technology, engineering, and math) industries, there are still not a lot of women doing handy work. This can make it difficult for teens and young girls to find role models after whom they can shape their career. However, there are certainly jobs available for women who are good working with their hands, as long as they apply and show an interest—and getting over the

(continued on the next page)

perception that only men capable of doing the jobs is the first step in the process.

One way women already working in handy industries help promote others is by reaching out and hosting seminars or lectures at which they talk to young women and girls who may be interested in entering the same field. It is worth checking with local colleges, universities, and community centers to see if there is a planned visit from a woman who works with her hands—and if there is nothing in the foreseeable future, a suggestion or request for such a speaker could go a long way.

Women are underrepresented in many industries that require manual labor, and speaking events can be a great way to spread the word about opportunities for girls in these fields.

Building More than Homes

Motivated teens can get training and experience working with their hands through a lot of different programs and organizations, many of which give back to their communities. One famous nationwide and international organization is Habitat for Humanity, which accepts volunteers to help build affordable housing for low-income families. Teenagers who are age sixteen and older can work on house construction

Habitat for Humanity is always looking for young volunteers. Working with charitable organizations like this is one way to gain experience and skills.

in their communities. Helping the less fortunate while getting hands-on building experience has inspired thousands of young people and given them a clear path forward in a handy industry.

Community organizations, either funded by charity or by local, state, and national government programs, often sponsor training and volunteer opportunities that concentrate on skilled trades.

Staying Up-to-Date

Beginning in the 2010s, there has been a movement around the United States to bring back job training in manufacturing. Due to the economic times, many manufacturers are actually finding it hard to fill skilled positions. This has resulted in the closure or downsizing of many businesses that still manufacture goods within the country. Industry groups everywhere have begun to work with governments, schools, and communities to prepare today's teens for tomorrow's jobs.

Many programs created through partnerships between businesses and communities offer teens opportunities to get free experience in skilled handy fields. Other organizations are hosting camps at which young people can learn handy skills and start networking with real businesses that are looking to hire youthful talent. Such programs are

Though many manufacturing companies in the United States have closed, there is an increasing number of opportunities for skilled laborers in these industries as they try to make a comeback.

popping up all over the country. One example is the Manufacturing Alliance of Bucks & Montgomery Counties, based in Pennsylvania. This consortium of companies targets young people who are good with their hands.

Many in the industry believe training programs can bring back U.S. leadership in manufacturing. Interested teens should seek out these kinds of programs to prepare them for jobs after high school that offer benefits and pay far better than starting positions in fast food or retail.

Pave Your Way

What if there are no openings in programs, nonprofits, or other opportunities in the area? Sometimes, it is necessary to make one's own. There are countless places to go and people to contact who might not even know they could use a motivated teen's help and expertise.

A young person experienced with audio and visual equipment might visit churches, community centers, and local meeting places to see if people need help with wiring or hooking up their meetings for sound or projection. They can charge inexpensive fees or do it for free, depending on the situation. Doing so every weekend can be a résumé-builder and add grateful contacts to someone's professional and social network. Word of mouth about one's work can lead to bigger, more profitable jobs.

Taking a walk around the neighborhood, an intrepid teen might observe buildings, fences, or other property that need repairs. Offering to paint old gray fencing, fix doors falling off their hinges, repair broken lawn furniture, and make other general home improvements are also options to find work opportunities locally.

CHAPTER FIVE

Play by the Rules

Though there are many reasons someone would want to do work with their hands, many fields and industries that involve this handy work can be risky or even dangerous. Power tools, such as saws and nail guns, cause thousands of injuries every year. Despite the risk involved in using these tools, however, they are an invaluable part of any handy worksite. For this reason, there are dozens of rules, regulations, and laws surrounding the professional or semi-professional use of such tools. It is important that anyone who wants to work with their hands understands these rules—not just for their own safety, but to make sure they do not break any local, state, or federal laws.

The consequences for not following standard operating procedure or regulatory practices for tools and machinery can be dangerous, harmful, and deadly. While it may save time to not wear safety glasses or a hard hat, for example, no amount of time saved is worth an eye or brain injury. In addition to the risk of physical harm, no company wants to be faced with a lawsuit for not providing proper training or enforcing the rules of a safe work environment. Businesses—from large corporations to self-employed teens—must always take proper care to reduce both types of risk if they plan to stay operational.

On top of safety concerns, it is also important for any employer, employee, or business owner to practice good business ethics. The topic of ethics is often debated and scrutinized, but there are some good basic rules to follow: follow the law and the rules, trust safety procedures, and always treat clients and coworkers with respect.

Laying Down the Law

Consult websites that cover state and federal labor laws for minors (anyone under eighteen) for a complete list of jobs and activities that are prohibited for any particular age group. Different, and sometimes quite complex, rules apply for those under fourteen, fourteen-to-fifteen-year-olds, and sixteen-to-eighteen-year-olds. In many states, for example, there are specific rules for different age groups working on farms or doing other agricultural work, especially those who work for their families.

Teens working with and around automobiles might be limited to particular tasks, such as cleaning, changing fluids, or inflating tires on cars, and are commonly prohibited from operating or working

Working on cars can be fun, challenging, and exciting for a handy teen, but it is important to follow the rules and regulations for auto repair workers.

near hydraulic lifts and other power equipment. The same goes for other fields that use power tools, such as carpentry, construction, plumbing, and waste management.

All U.S. states have minimum age requirements for teen workers. In most cases, someone must be at least fourteen years old to work. Rules are often stricter for those under the age of sixteen. Federal and state laws also limit how many hours a week—and at what times—a teen can work.

During the Massachusetts school year, for example, teen workers under the age of sixteen can work eighteen hours per week—only three hours each day on school days and eight hours daily on weekends and holidays. During summer vacations, they can work up to a maximum of six days every week and for forty total hours. Older teens can often only work until certain times at night. Many laws prohibit those under the age of eighteen from working with specific types of heavy machinery, too. Researching these details is important for both teens and their parents before applying for any job.

Safety Training

Most employers or supervisors, especially those involved in physical labor, will know what safety equipment is needed on the job and will provide it. Still, one should always research these details by obtaining a thorough job description before starting work and make sure that the proper gear is distributed. Common safety gear and clothing includes safety goggles, ear protection, sturdy gloves, respirators, face shields and masks (for welding sparks and foreign matter), steel-toe boots, long-sleeve shirts, overalls, and fluorescent vests for work sites.

For teens running their own business, locating and supplying safety equipment and clothing may be a bit trickier. More research is needed, and they need to purchase or obtain this gear themselves, rather than relying on others. Parents and other

Power tools are commonplace in manual labor industries, so workers must always be sure to use the appropriate eye, ear, and hand protection, as well as following any additional safety rules.

trusted family members are the first people to ask about the necessary gear for any job or task.

Thousands of workers are injured or killed on the job every year. Some tragedies are unpredictable, but many are preventable, arising from carelessness or poor planning and preparation. Unfortunately, some companies endanger their employees (including older, experienced ones) when they ignore age limits for young workers.

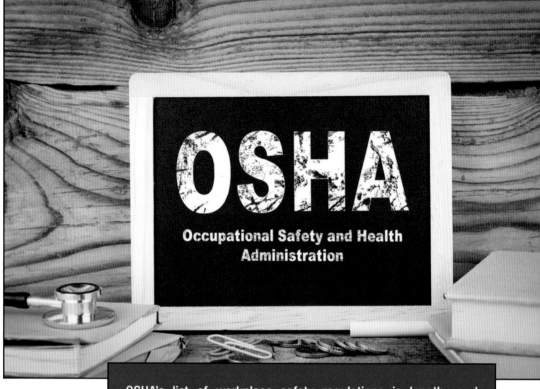

OSHA's list of workplace safety regulations is lengthy and comprehensive. Workers and employers that do not follow these guidelines can find themselves in a lot of trouble.

The Occupational Health and Safety Administration (OSHA), a division of the United States Department of Labor, is the organization in charge of regulating workplace safety rules and making sure businesses are in compliance with all safety laws. Its website offers a huge quantity of information for young workers, including a list of rights and explanations of safety procedures that should be followed at all kinds of worksites.

STAYING CAREFUL

One of the most important things any young worker can do is be informed—and this is especially true if that person is working with their hands. While doing research before accepting or starting a particular job is a good place to start, being safe on the job is an ongoing procedure. One part of that process is asking questions of supervisors or more experienced employees. The more time someone has spent on the job, the more tips they have likely picked up. Asking a lot of questions about safety procedures can keep everyone safe. OSHA's young workers portal lists several crucial rights and responsibilities for workers in potentially hazardous jobsites:

- "You have the right to ask questions if you don't understand instructions or if something seems unsafe."
- "You have the right to exercise your workplace safety rights without retaliation or discrimination."
- "Your employer must provide training about workplace hazards and required safety gear."
- "Your employer must tell you where to get answers to your safety or health questions."

Watch Your Own Back

Employees, their employers, and self-employed workers should be aware of many of the common causes and types of safety hazards and work to limit them as much as possible. Falling is one of the most common causes of death or injury, and painters, roofers, tree-service technicians, carpenters, and many others working high up must be mindful of its dangers.

Workers of all types must also be aware of electrical equipment, exposed wires, and other shock hazards. Operators of heavy machinery and

Doing electrical work, whether on cars, homes, or utilities, can be dangerous, but there are ways to reduce the risk by using safety equipment, such as a voltmeter.

vehicles, and those near them, need to stay alert to avoid crushing or otherwise injuring colleagues.

Self-employed teens, who may be unsupervised much of the time, should also be careful when using hammers and nails and sharp items like sheet metal, knives, and other tools. Unplugging electric tools or items when not in use can help prevent shock risks.

Depending on the job, handy workers likely use some kind of tools or equipment. It is important that they read all instruction manuals or packaging instructions, no matter how simple a tool or piece of equipment might seem. Before starting work using anything, ask a trusted, knowledgeable adult for proper instructions about its use. Never use any unfamiliar or new tool for the first time without supervision from someone experienced. It might take several tries before someone is comfortable with new gear.

The same is true for the larger environment of the workplace or work site. Proper training or instruction in how to use and work around ladders, scaffolding, and other structures goes a long way in keeping everyone safe.

Ultimately, the greatest piece of safety equipment anyone has is always available: their own head. Be alert and think through every action and its consequences when doing physical labor. Safety also means never picking up anything too heavy to lift, staying hydrated—especially in hot weather—and avoiding exhaustion. Teens should always alert a supervisor if they feel dizzy or disoriented, or if they are injured in any way, however minor.

Know the Limits

As they explore the various opportunities out there, handy teens will discover that being patient and knowing their limits is better than rushing and overextending themselves. Taking on a job that one cannot perform is not only bad business, but can also be dangerous. A teen may be able to fix someone's remote control, but that does not mean they can safely fix a malfunctioning wall socket. Taking unnecessary risks can end up causing embarrassment and even injury.

Instead, a step-by-step approach will yield the best results. Taking the time to build skills means starting small and climbing up the ladder. This is important not only in one's own private business, but especially if one works for others. It is arguably even more necessary in physical and skilled labor because such money-making opportunities leave little room for error.

Of course, one will make more mistakes at the beginning of the journey into the hands-on workforce; this is expected, necessary, and one of the main ways to learn. As a worker learns and gains experience, that she or he will obtain better-paying and more interesting work.

Nothing Underhanded Here

Teens doing any kind of work must also abide by all local, state, and federal tax regulations that apply to them and make sure to file taxes every year. Employees will have any applicable taxes taken out for them from every paycheck. They should save their pay stubs and make sure to get a W-2 every year for each employer they worked for. It does not hurt to review deductions with parents to make sure that all the numbers add up.

Self-employed teens will have to figure out their own payments, which are owed to the government as a self-employment tax. Keeping all receipts or records of any money spent as overhead for the business is crucial, as is tracking all incoming money. In most cases, income earned in cash must be tracked carefully, too. Checking with parents and official government websites, and even consulting an accountant or tax lawyer will help working teens figure out their income reporting responsibilities. It is not worth the risk to get into trouble with the law. In some cases, someone who hides his or her income can also put clients and customers at risk.

The Golden Rule(s)

Working teens should also be mindful of others in everything they do. In the workplace, this means taking responsibility for mistakes or failures and not passing blame to others. Bosses and coworkers rely on workers doing their jobs correctly. Being dishonest can even lead to accidents or injury for others, not to mention causing employers to lose money or time. Dishonest workers might be fired and will not have as many opportunities for future work.

Self-employed teens must be honest and fair with those who rely on their work, products, and services. Always do what is agreed on, without cutting corners. Badly made furniture can break and injure someone. Overcharging for sloppy work or services will anger and disappoint customers. A bad work reputation gets around quickly in the age of social media—but a good reputation can spread just as fast.

A Hard-Knock Life

The manual arts are not for everyone, even if people have the talent. Many jobs can be physically demanding. Years of working with their hands expose many individuals to occupational hazards. Certain repetitive motions done over the years are known to cause the painful condition known as carpal tunnel syndrome. The risk of injury, exhaustion, aches, pains, and other symptoms of physical labor are also things to consider. Those with physical limitations should also think about how these limitations can affect their career progress.

The benefits of being handy, however, far outweigh the dangers of pursuing this lifestyle. Millions of people have found that the manual arts are good for their souls, as well as their bank accounts. Handy teens will gain discipline, independence, and satisfaction from money-making opportunities that are just around the corner.

GLOSSARY

apprenticeship A work arrangement in which a novice worker learns a skill or trade under an experienced practitioner.

bookkeeping The practice of maintaining detailed records of business transactions.

contractor A person in the skilled trades that agrees to a contract with a client to provide labor or other services.

DIY Acronym for "do it yourself," describing a self-reliant philosophy of working or making things.

downsizing The act of reducing the number of jobs in a company; commonly done to increase profitability during tough economic times.

entrepreneur A person who starts his or her own business.

ethics Principles that guide the behavior of individuals and groups, including business relationships.

handy Describing someone who is good at working with their hands.

internship A working arrangement in which a novice worker, often unpaid, receives practical training in his or her field.

intrepid Describing someone who is adventurous and ambitious.

invoice A formal bill or record for goods or
services provided, stating the amount of
money owed.

manual arts Any creative activity involving
manufacturing or the skilled trades.

manufacturing An industry in which goods
are produced.

masons Skilled tradespeople who work with stone
or brick in construction.

networking Reaching out to and connecting with
potential clients or other businesses.

OSHA Abbreviation for the Occupational Safety
and Health Administration, which regulates
worker safety and health in the United States.

outsourcing In the context of the labor market,
the process by which companies obtain
labor and service in foreign nations, rather
than domestically.

recession A period of time during which an
economy is weak and the general population
has less money.

résumé A document listing work and life
experiences; used as part of a job application.

scaffolding Temporary structures put up on
the outside of buildings to support workers
and equipment.

skilled trade A craft or business that involves manual labor, in which someone receives specialized training to develop abilities over time.

vocational Refers to occupation or employment and specifically to a type of education that prepares students for a job in the manual arts.

W-2 A form that an employer must send to an employee and the Internal Revenue Service at the end of the year; reports a worker's annual wages and the amount of taxes withheld from his or her paycheck.

FURTHER READING

Books

Culp, Jennifer. *Using Computer Science in Automotive Careers*. New York, NY: Rosen YA, 2019.

Fry, Ronald W. *101 Great Answers to the Toughest Interview Questions*. Hawthorne, NJ: Career Press, 2018.

Kitts, W.L. *Great Jobs in the Skilled Trades*. San Diego, CA: ReferencePoint Press, 2019.

Labrecque, Ellen. *Carpenter*. Ann Arbor, MI: Cherry Lake Publishing, 2017.

Mapua, Jeff. *A Career as an Electrician*. New York, NY: Rosen YA, 2019.

Wolny, Philip. *Getting a Job in the Construction Industry*. New York, NY: Rosen Publishing, 2017.

Websites

ApprenticeshipUSA
apprenticeshipusa.workforcegps.org
This site offers valuable information about landing an apprenticeship in many different industries; it also has a forums section in which users can join community discussions about apprenticeships.

Teens4Hire
www.teens4hire.org
This website offers both local job listings for teens looking for work and informational postings about the labor market.

Young Workers—You Have Rights!
www.osha.gov/youngworkers/workers.html
This portal, accessed through the official OSHA website, features a lot of information about workplace safety, specifically tailored for young job seekers.

BIBLIOGRAPHY

Associated Press. "More than Seven in 10 US Teens Jobless in Summer." Fox News, June 12, 2012. https://www.foxnews.com/us/more-than-seven -in-10-us-teens-jobless-in-summer.

Butrymowicz, Sarah. "Push for Career-Technical Education Meets Parent Resistance." Hechinger Report, July 17, 2012. http://hechingerreport .org/content/push-for-career-technical -education-meets-parent-resistance_9015.

Canal, Emily. "How This 16-Year-Old Founder Build a $600,000 Bow Tie Business." Inc., November 13, 2017. https://www.inc.com/emily-canal/how-this -young-entrepreneur-got-the-best-deal-on-shark -tank-with-daymond-john.html.

Copeland, Julie. "Top 10 Most Common Workplace Injuries." Arbill. Retrieved April 14, 2019. https://www.arbill.com/arbill-safety-blog/bid /202877/Top-10-Most-Common-Workplace -Injuries.

Crawford, Matthew B. "The Case for Working with Your Hands." *New York Times Magazine*, May 21, 2009. http://www.nytimes.com/2009/05/24 /magazine/24labor-t.html.

Feyder, Susan. "Turning Manufacturing into Women's Work." *Star Tribune*, May 12, 2012. http://www.startribune.com/business /151187325.html.

Gralla, Joan. "Teen Unemployment Persists in Summer 2012, as Teens Compete with Adults for Low-Wage Jobs." *Huffington Post*, June 16, 2012. http://www.huffingtonpost.com/2012/06/16/teen-unemployment-summer-2012_n_1602254.html.

Gross, Ashley and Jon Marcus. "High-Paying Trade Jobs Sit Empty, While High School Grads Line Up For University." NPR, April 25, 2018. https://www.npr.org/sections/ed/2018/04/25/605092520/high-paying-trade-jobs-sit-empty-while-high-school-grads-line-up-for-university.

Kapitan, Claire. "Why Manufacturing's Not Cool." IndustryWeek, March 1, 2019. https://www.industryweek.com/leadership/why-manufacturing-s-not-cool.

Klein, Karen E. "Worker Shortage? Teach Teens Manufacturing Skills." *Business Week*, July 5, 2012. http://www.businessweek.com/articles/2012-07-05/struggling-to-find-skilled-workers-manufacturers-target-young.

Knisely, Alex. "Young Entrepreneur Hart Main, 17, Owns Successful Candle Business." *Times Reporter*, July 21, 2015. https://www.timesreporter.com/article/20150720/news/150729951.

Manufacturing Industry Advisor. "The Skills
    Gap in the Manufacturing Industry and What
    We Can Do About It." Foley & Lardner LLP,
    September 13, 2018. https://www.foley.com/the
    -skills-gap-in-the-manufacturing-industry-and
    -what-we-can-do-about-it-09-13-2018.

Occupational Safety and Health Administration.
    "Safe Work for Young Workers." United States
    Department of Labor. Retrieved April 10, 2019.
    https://www.osha.gov/youngworkers
    /workers.html.

Rogers, Kate. "Manufacturing Is Firing on All
    Cylinders, but a Lack of Skilled Workers Is
    Squeezing the Sector." CNBC, September 7,
    2018. https://www.cnbc.com/2018/09/07/
    manufacturing-is-firing-on-all-cylinders-but-a
    -lack-of-skilled-workers-is-squeezing-the
    -sector.html.

Toren, Matthew. "10 Awesome Business Ideas for
    Teen Entrepreneurs." Business Insider, February
    16, 2011. http://www.businessinsider.com/10
    -awesome-business-ideas-for-the-teen
    -entrepreneur-2011-2?op=1.

YoungWorkers.org. "Teen Workers." National
    Young Workers Safety Resource Center.
    Retrieved April 17, 2019. http://youngworkers
    .org/rights/teenworkers.

INDEX